Italy 1965: A Pocket Sexual Revolution

Antonio A. Casilli

The history of Italian adult comics begins like a novel. It was a dark and stormy night in the winter of 1965. Renzo Barbieri, who was working as a PR for the car producer Ferrari, was travelling by train, on his way home to Milan after a business trip. Just to kill time, he bought a copy of Diabolik, a thriller comic which was having a wide commercial success. After reading it through, he said to himself quite simply: "I could write myself a story of this kind hands down." A few months later, in April 1966, Barbieri founded the now mythic publishing house Editrice Sessantasei (Sixty-six Editions), which launched an amazing series of fumetti sexy tascabili "pocket sex-comics".

These booklets told of the vicissitudes of some sexually liberated heroines who moved through adventures while indulging in a wide range of erotic interludes in which they experimented every imaginable perversion. The stories (in quite different genres—noirs, horror novels, historical dramas, spy stories, fairytales) usually ran around 130 pages. The art was strictly black-and-white, sometimes hastily, sometimes excellently drawn. The covers, however, were in full colour, and extremely well designed. Readers, raised in the Italian respectable catholic environment, found a whole world of exciting, yet discrete, transgressions. That's it, *discrete*: the great advantage of those little books was their 13 x 18cm format. People could buy them at the local newstand and comfortably hide them in their pocket. For a few coins they could carry home with them the stories of the provocative swordswoman Angelica, the perverse "She-Devil" Lucifera, the malicious "Little Witch" Maghella, the insatiable empress Messalina and the violent Madame Brutal.

Such series were smash hits for those years' readers. They fostered the ideals of sexual liberation, new habits, and lifestyles. And they went hand-in-hand with the real sexual revolution, the one Italian youth were experiencing those very same years. That revolution was known as the "European '68 movement." College students were invading the streets to protest against bourgeois society and its values of hypocritical respectability and conservative conformism.

Often the confrontations were physical, rather than ideological: strikes, public demonstrations, happenings, sit-ins often ended in police repression. Sure, those young Italian demonstrators carried Karl Marx's Manifesto in their right pockets, but they had copies of Oltretomba "Zombie" or Jungla the African Virgin in their left one.

Almost every barbershop, school, and neighbourhood bar had five or six issues of those fumettazzi "comic hits" tucked away in some hidden corner. They were spreading like an epidemic. Their success was instantaneous. Each month new titles were delivered to the newstands: Barbieri alone counted more than 6000 start-ups in his long career. Sales were sky-rocketing, moralists were more and more scandalised, and publishers were often reported to justice: Barbieri collected 103 lawsuits, all vindicated. Sexy comics became an integrating part of Italian pop culture, because they expressed the will to break taboos, to "prohibit prohibitions"—a need Italian younger generations were increasingly urged by. Those comics spoke straight to the reader's body, desires, and fantasies. They were not all-the-way pornographic comics; erotic scenes were self-censored by shadow and blur effects. They were, however, the first to deal with such themes as male and female homosexuality (in Sukia and Biancaneve "Snow White"), free love (in Pompea and Jolanda d'Almaviva), and sadomasochism (in Goldrake, or in the cult-comics Sadik and Masokis).

Not surprisingly, pocket sex-comics were also an important testing ground for major talents in Italian comics. The stories had excellent plots, thanks to scriptwriters such as Giorgio Cavedon or Alberto Ongaro. The artwork pushed to real heights of bravura with cartoonists like Leone Frollo and Milo Manara. Not to mention covers, by several skilled professionals from "illustration studios" (the most relevant was the Rome-based Studio Rosi).

Soon it was clear that those comics not only reflected social changes, but actually gave shape to them. Sex-comic heroines, for instance, influenced fashion. For years, Italian girls wore high boots like Isabella or long hair dressed like Jacula. Furthermore, these characters also changed the way of thinking gender relations, family ties, and the role of women in society. It is worth saying that their nerve and non-conformism gave Italian women the strength to fight for their own rights during the women liberation season.

After that, in the second half of the '70s, sex-comics became darker, less light-hearted, more violent. Horror series started being populated by femmes fatales with scaring names. That new wave in comics echoed the growing discomfort spreading among men towards emancipated women, who were always described as vampires (women who contaminate manhood with their infected desires) or as castrating amazons (dominatrixes revenging themselves on male inadequacies). No one was alarmed by the violence in adult comics, because Italian society itself had become unbearably violent. Student protests had turned in armed hostilities. Thus, pocket sex-comics were a compulsory reading for young Italian subversives: pages of Lando and Il Tromba "The Lecher" were used by revolutionary organisations as eccentric claims for outrages (a technique known as détournement - scribbling out the text and writing extremist slogans in the dialog balloons). Utopia turned into the nightmare of the "bullet years." Innocent infringements, sexual freedom, and experiments in alternative lifestyles were knocked down either by terrorists madness, or, even worse, by police and criminal justice repression that in a few years, swept away the entire counter-culture movement. That was the period of restoration, when everybody gave up their efforts to change bourgeois society.

Sex-comics echoed this atmosphere of delusion and consummated catastrophe. The fantastic tales of the previous years gave way to tasteless sensationalism after the American "exploitation" model. Thus the Attualità "True Stories" series was born : Attualità Nera "Black Tales," Attualità Proibita "Forbidden Tales," Attualità Violenta "Violent Tales" were inspired by real crimes. Serial killers, dismemberments, psychopaths, rapes, heroin addiction, the Mafia—a whole repertoire of social ills rapid-fire. Stories in the '80s

proposed pessimistic visions of life, society and, alas, sex. The portrayal of sex in particular became increasingly sick, ever more tied to the idea of death, guilt and suffering.

In this period, the country was experiencing a wave of sheer moralist regurgitation. Even though sex-comics were showing for the first time "hardcore" graphic details (penetrations, male genitals and sperm), that meant nothing. The sense of common decency was not jeopardised. On the contrary, sexual liberation was by that time a lost battle in Italy. Artists were allowed to represent everything—"leaving nothing to imagination"—because imagination itself was irredeemably censored. Imagination, that held such power for the youth of '68, in the '80s proved no good even as pulp for masturbation. Between the end of the '80s and the beginning of the '90s, production of pocket sex-comics ceased completely. Sure, various reprints, anthologies, and paperbacks were commercialised, but the golden age was definitely over. No one was interested in well-written stories anymore. Moreover, comics could not compete against photographic porn and hardcore videos.

That's why they disappeared from newstands and became mere curiosities for "trash" collectors. Like Red Army badges in Russia or Ed Wood's films in the US, today sex-comics in Italy have become the epitome of a world that no longer exists. One last sad remark: my own personal opinion is that adult pocketbooks (along with all associated potential for social fantasy and sexual creativity) followed such a pitiable path, just because of their small and discrete size. Reducing major cultural changes to little 13 x 18cm booklets is not a good strategy at all. A sexual revolution should not be relegated in a pocket. Otherwise one risks to forget extracting it at the right moment.

The lesson this whole story teaches is that revolutions must always be *a few centimetres bigger* than the pocket supposed to contain them. They should pop up all the time, so that one never forgets they're there—ready to burst.

mors tua, vita mea

イタリア1965年：ポケット版の性革命

アントニオ・A・カッシーリ

イタリアにおける成人漫画の歴史は、それ自体が一編の小説のように幕を開ける。1965年、荒れ模様の冬の夜のこと、フェラーリ社の広報を担当していたレンツォ・バルビエリは、ミラノへと向かう出張帰りの列車に乗っていた。退屈しのぎに買ったのが、そのころ大売れしていたスリラー漫画『ダイアボリック』の一冊。読み終わってみて、彼はこう思わずにいられなかった---「こんなのなら、自分にだって楽勝で描ける」。そして数カ月たった1966年4月のこと、バルビエリはいまや伝説となった出版社エディトリチェ・セッサンタセイ（66書籍）を立ち上げた。その最初の刊行物がフュメッティ・セクシー・タスカビーリ（ポケット版成人漫画）と題された、驚異のシリーズである。

ストーリーはいずれも、セックスに対して自由な考えを持つ女主人公たちが、さまざまな冒険に立ち向かいつつ、その過程でありとあらゆる倒錯的性行為に耽るというもの。ホラー、ノワール、歴史もの、スパイもの、童話風と幅広いジャンルにわたる内容で、通常130ページほどのつくりになっていた。作画はかならず白黒と決まっていて、粗いタッチのものから精緻な画風までいろいろだったが、表紙はいつもフルカラーで、印象的なデザインを特徴とする。

イタリア伝統の厳しいカトリック環境で育ってきた読者にとって成人漫画は、まさしく興奮と悪徳の悦びに満ちた、ひそやかな新世界を発見する思いだった。そう、ひそやかさ。13×18センチというその小ぶりな版型に、実は成功の秘密が隠されていたのである。どこのニューズスタンドでも購入でき、洋服のポケットに楽にしまえるサイズ。挑発的な女剣士アンジェリカや、悪魔の倒錯女王ルシフェーラ、意地悪魔女マゲーラ、貪欲女王メッサリーナ、残忍なマダム・ブルータルといった魅力的な物語を、たった硬貨数枚で家に持ち帰ることができたのだ。

こうしたシリーズは、当時の読者たちに大受けした。成人漫画は性革命や、新たなライフスタイルのアイデアを育む原動力となり、まさに同時期にイタリアの若者たちが体験しつつあった、現実の性革命と手を携えるかたちで発展していった。当時の変革はいま、「ヨーロッパ68年ムーヴメント」として知られている。学生が街頭に繰り出し、ブルジョワ社会の偽善的道徳観念、保守迎合主義に激しい異議を唱えた、あの騒乱の季節である。対決はしばしば、イデオロギーというよりも肉体的なぶつかりあいになり、ストライキ、大衆を巻き込んだデモ、ハプニング、座り込みなど、多くの行動が警察権力の介入を招く事態へと発展する。

そしてイタリアの怒れる若者たちは右手にカール・マルクスの共産党宣言を携え、しかし左手には『オルトレトンバ』（ゾンビー）や、『アフリカの処女ジャングラ』といった漫画の一冊があったのだった。

床屋、学校、バールといった場所にはかならず、フュメッツィ（漫画本）が何冊か、隅っこに隠してあった。その成功はほとんど瞬時のできごとであり、広まりかたはあたかも伝染病のようだった。なにしろ毎月、新しい号がニューズスタンドに届けられる。バルビエリだけでも、その長い歴史で6000号以上を数えている。驚異的な売り上げに保守層は憤慨し、出版社は司法の舞台に引きずり出されることともなった。たとえばバルビエリは、すべて無罪を勝ち取ったものの、103回におよぶ訴訟を起こされている。

こうして成人漫画は、イタリアのポップ文化に欠かせない要素となっていく。因習を打ち破り、「禁ずることを禁ずる」意志を表現しているために。実際、それこそがイタリアの若い世代を駆り立てたからである。漫画は読者の肉体に、欲望に、そして幻想に直接語りかけた。官能的な場面は陰影やぼかしなどで自主検閲されていたものの、『スキア』、『ビアンカネーヴェ』（白雪姫）に登場した男女ともどもの同性愛、フリー・ラヴ（『ポンペア』、『ジョランダ・ダルマヴィヴァ』）、サドマゾヒズム（『ゴールドレイク』、またカルトとなった『サディック』や『マゾキス』）といった主題を扱う、最初の媒体ともなった。

また当然のことながらポケット版成人漫画は、イタリアの漫画家にとって重要な実験の場ともなった。ジョルジオ・カヴェドンやアルベルト・オンガロといった、才能豊かな新人によってストーリーが磨き上げられ、作画のほうもレオーネ・フロオロやミロ・マナーラなどにより完成度の極みに達する。もちろんいくつかのイラストレーション・スタジオ（そのもっとも代表的なものは、ローマのストゥディオ・ロッシである）による、表紙デザインも忘れてはならない。

こうした漫画本はまもなく、現実に起こりつつある社会変容を反映するのみならず、変革にある方向性を与えうるものであることが明らかになってきた。セックス漫画の女主人公たちの、たとえばファッション業界への影響を見てみよう。イタリアの女の子たちにはイザベッラのようなロングブーツや、ジャキュラのようなロングヘアーが長いことお気に入りだった。さらにこうした主人公たちは、イタリア社会のジェンダーや家族関係、社会における女性の役割などに関する考え方をも変えて

" Your death is my life " (in Latin)
おまえの死は私の生

L. 250

いく。女性解放運動の歩みの中で、彼女らの大胆で妥協を許さない行動スタイルが、イタリア女性たちにみずから戦うちからを与えたのである。

70年代後半になるにしたがい成人漫画は明るさを失い、暴力を基調とした暗い物語へと変質していく。おぞましい名前のファム・ファタールを主人公にした、ホラーものが人気を博すようになった。こうした新たな傾向は、解放された女性たちに対する、男性側のとまどいを反映したものでもある。作品中で女主人公は女吸血鬼（邪悪な情欲によって男を破滅させる女性）、アマゾネス（能力の劣る男への怒りから変身を遂げた女王戦士）などとして描かれるようになる。

しかし成人漫画の内包する暴力性を、憂う声は聞かれることがなかった。イタリア社会そのものが、耐えがたいまでの暴力に満ちていたからである。学生の反抗は武器による対決へとかたちを変え、ポケット版成人漫画がイタリアの若き不穏分子にとって必読書となる。その過程で『ランドゥ』や『イル・トロンバ』（好色家）のページが、革命組織によってエキセントリックな怒りのメッセージとして使われることともなった（これはデトゥルヌマン＝転回と呼ばれる技法で、あるカットから吹き出しの文字を消し去り、そこに自分たちの過激なスローガンを書き入れる方法）。ユートピアはいまや「銃弾の季節」と名づけられた悪夢に変節する。無邪気な造反や性の解放、オルタナティブなライフスタイルの実験であったものが、テロリストの狂気か、さらに悪い場合には警察や司法権力によって、たった数年のあいだにカウンターカルチャーの胎動を吹き飛ばしてしまったのである。復古の時代が、社会変革への望みを捨て去るときがきた。

幻滅ムードを反映するかたちで、セックス漫画は崩壊への道を辿りはじめる。かつての物語性豊かな内容は、アメリカ式の「エクスプロイテーション」・スタイルに影響され、悪趣味なセンセーショナリズムへと堕落していった。そして生まれたのがアチュアリタ（実話）シリーズである。『アチュアリタ・ネーラ』（黒の実話）、『アチュアリタ・プロイビタ』（禁断実話）、『アチュアリタ・ヴィオレンタ』（暴力実話）など、すべて実際の犯罪に基づいたものだった。連続殺人、手足切断、精神異常、強姦、ヘロイン中毒、マフィア・・・さまざまな社会病理のかたちが、続々登場するようになった。80年代のストーリーは人生や社会、そしてセックスについてまで、悲観的なヴィジョンを描き出すようになる。とりわけセックスの描きかたはますます病的に、ますます死や罪悪や苦痛をともなうものへと変質していった。

この時期のイタリアは、道徳的な回帰ともいうべき潮流のただ中にあった。成人漫画には史上初めて「ハードコア」な描写が登場するようになったが（挿入、男性性器、精液など）、それも役に立たなかった。公衆道徳の概念は揺るがず、それどころか性解放に向けた戦いは、ここに至って負け戦となることがはっきりしてきた。アーティストはなんでも描くことが許された---「なにものをもイマジネーションにゆだねることなく」。しかしイマジネーションそのものが、もはや修復不可能なまでに検閲されてしまったのである。68年の若者たちにあれほどの力を与えてくれたイマジネーションというものが、80年代においてはもはや、マスターベーション用の誌面としてさえ機能しなくなったのだ。

80年代終わりから90年代はじめにかけて、ポケット版の成人漫画はまったく出版されなくなる。もちろんさまざまな復刊やアンソロジー、文庫化されたものが市場に出回ったが、黄金時代は完全に終わりを迎えたのである。もはやだれも、程度の高いストーリーには興味を持たなくなっていた。それどころか漫画というもの自体が、ポルノ写真やハードコア・ビデオにかなわなくなっていたのだった。

こうして成人漫画はニューズスタンドから姿を消し、変わった趣味のコレクターたちの収集品と化した。ロシアの共産党バッジや、エド・ウッド監督の映画のように、イタリアの成人漫画はもはや存在しない世界の縮図となっている。そして最後に、悲観的な考察をひとつ。私個人としては、ポケット版の成人向け書籍が（それに関連した社会的幻想や性的創造力とともに）哀れな末路を辿ったのは、その小さくて隠しやすいサイズそのものに原因があったのではないかと考えている。重要な社会変革を13×18センチなどという小さな本に閉じこめるのは、まったく効果的な戦略ではない。性の革命というものは、ポケットなどに追いやられるべきものではないのだ。そうでなければ、いちばん大事なときに引っぱり出すのを忘れてしまうではないか。

成人漫画の興亡から導き出される教訓は、革命とはつねに、ポケットに収まるよりも「何センチか大きく」なくてはならないということだ。ポケットからはみ出し、いつなんどきも忘れようがないもの。そしていつも爆発寸前の状態で、そこにあるということ。

翻訳：都築響一

FUME
PER ADU
L. 80

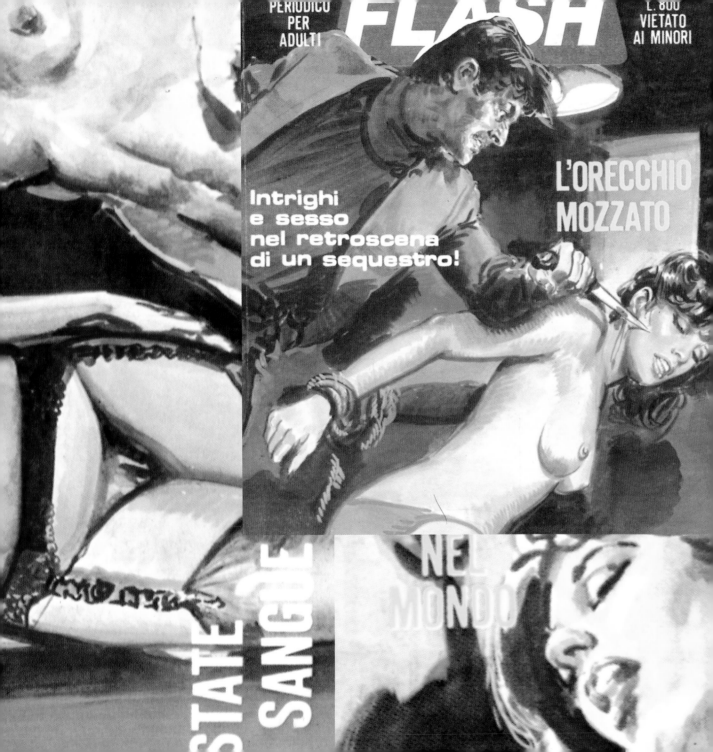

PERIODICO PER ADULTI

FLASH

L. 800 VIETATO AI MINORI

L'ORECCHIO MOZZATO

Intrighi e sesso nel retroscena di un sequestro!

STATE SANGUE

NEL MONDO

FLASH

L. 1000
VIETATO
AI MINORI

PECCATI
SEGRETI

" Secret sin "
When your secret lover dies in bed
before your eyes...
＂秘められた罪＂あなたの愛人が
ベッドの中で悶絶えるのを目の当たりにしたとき…

Quando l'amante
segreto ti muore
nel letto...

GIAL

" Infernal lovers "
Chilling murder on a gangland ba
『地獄の恋人たち』 裏通りの惨劇

GLI AMANTI INI

gghiacciante delitto
sfondo
malavita

CRIMEN
NEL
MONDO

GIALLA

VIETATO
AI MINORI

"The killing of a vicious man
A Naples man disappears. Sizzling intrigue and love stories...
Blood and mystery in the troubled shadows of the Napoli Mafia
【殺された悪党】
消えたナポリの男。陰謀、そして愛。ナポリ・マフィアの影に血と謎

UCCISIONE
DI UN VIZIOSO

Cittadino insospettabile
coltiva vizi segreti

CRIMEN
NEL
MONDO

BASTA
ALL'IM

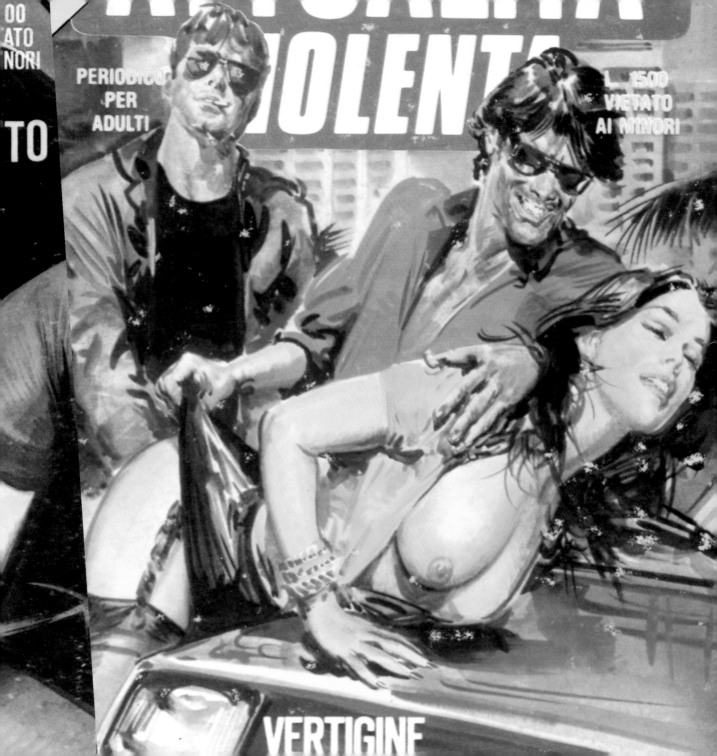

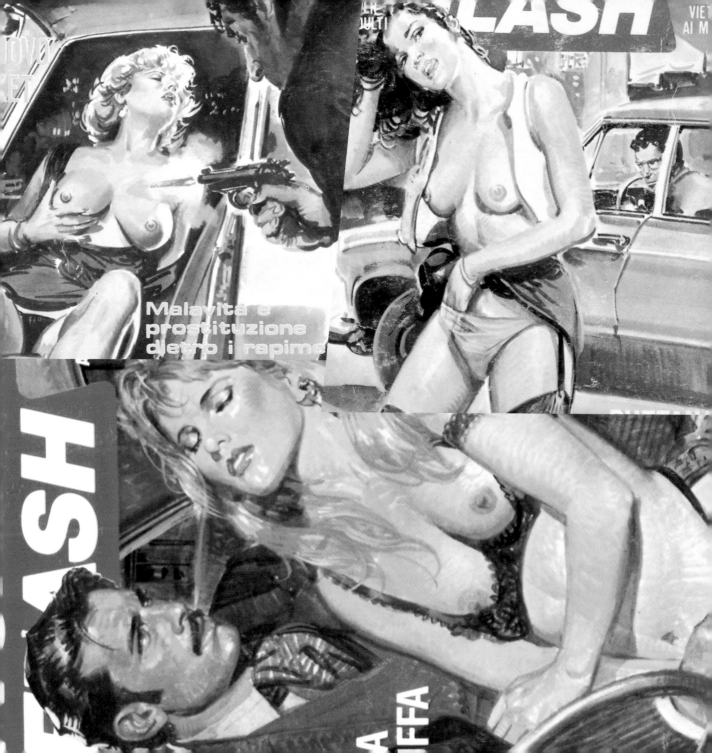

L. 300
VIETATO
AI MINORI

PROIBIT

PERIODICO - PER - ADULTI

L'OSCENO AMANTE

" The phantom porno magazines "
Subscriptions fraud of non-existent sinful magazines
『魔のポルノ雑誌』
存在しない背徳雑誌の予約販売詐欺

SEXY RIVISTE
FANTASMA

Abbonamenti truffa
a giornali peccaminosi
inesistenti...

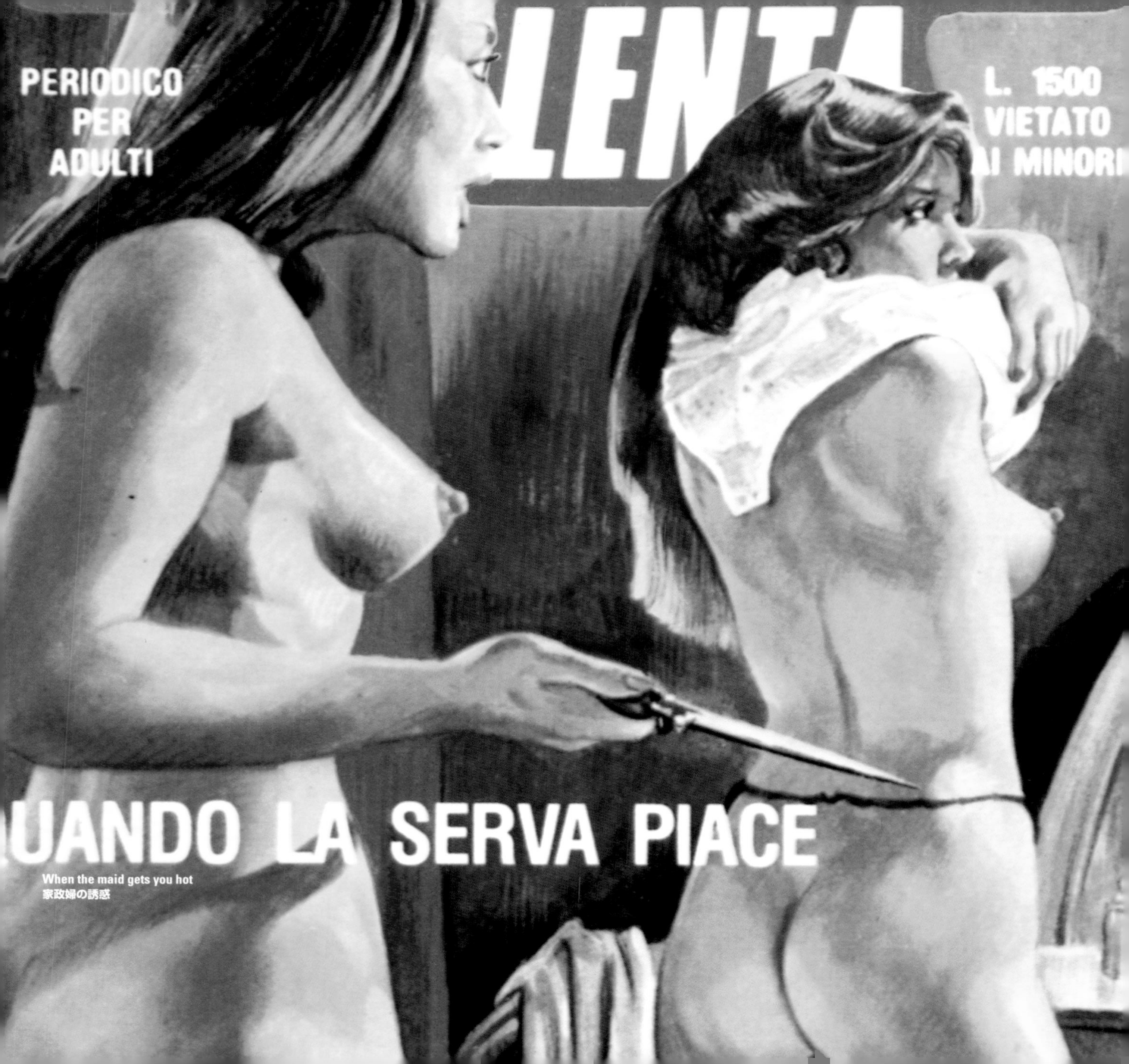

When the maid gets you hot
家政婦の誘惑

MARTELLO
PER UCCIDERE

A hammer to kill
殺人ハンマー

PERIODICO PER ADULTI

L. 1500
VIETATO AI MINORI

L. 15
VIETA
AI MI

Sesso
terrore

RICORDATI
DI UCCIDERE

BRAVO

A NERA AUTO
ELLA MORTE

The black car of death
死を運ぶ黒い車

VIETATO AI MINORI
L. 600

ATTUALITÀ FLASH

L. 1000
VIETATO
AI MINORI

FOTO

FINO
ALL' ULTIMA CO

"Sizzling photos"
For a young girl to pose naked can be dangerous!
Filthy speculators wait in ambush
「危険な写真」
裸でポーズをとる若い女に次々に迫る危険!
卑劣な撮影師が彼らを待ち伏せする

Per una ragazza
posare nuda
può essere
pericoloso!
Turpi speculatori
sono in
...
...ACRATORE

TUALITA

ITALITA

PROIBITA

TTUUAALIITÀ

TÀ DI SESSO

farsi violentare
a costo di pagare...

"Sex obsession"
She loves to be raped, even if she has to pay
「セックスの妄想」
金を払ってでもレイプされたいと願う女

FUMET

L. 35

Storie di mostri e di vampiri

NGUINA

e di mostri e di vampir

FUMET
PER ADU
L. 20
BELGIO 20 FB
FRANCIA 2 F
GERMANIA 1,60
INGHILTERRA 14
SVIZZERA 2 F

LA LEGGENDA
DI BAMBARA

Stories of monsters and vampires
ばけ物と吸血鬼の物語

il bastardo

VON KANINEN IL VAM

NEL NOME DEL PADRINO, UCCIDI!

In the name of the godfather, kill!
ゴッドファーザーの名の下に、殺せ！

FUMETTI PER ADULTI

L. 200

N2

EPISODIO COMPLETO

esurrezione
FUMETTI
PER ADULTI
L. 200
DI 16
rombo rosso
colore
EPISODIO
L. 400
publi strip ristampa

colore

EPISODIO
COMPLETO
A COLORI

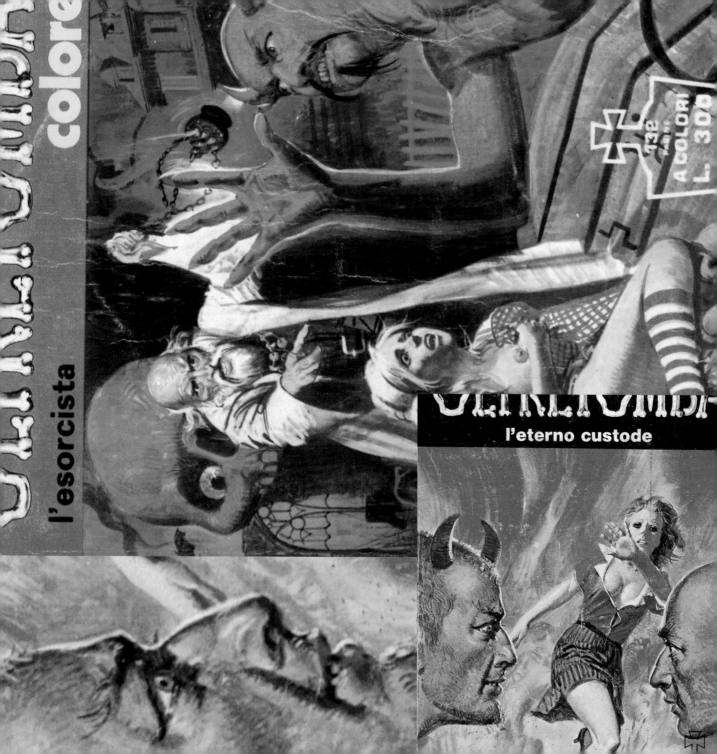

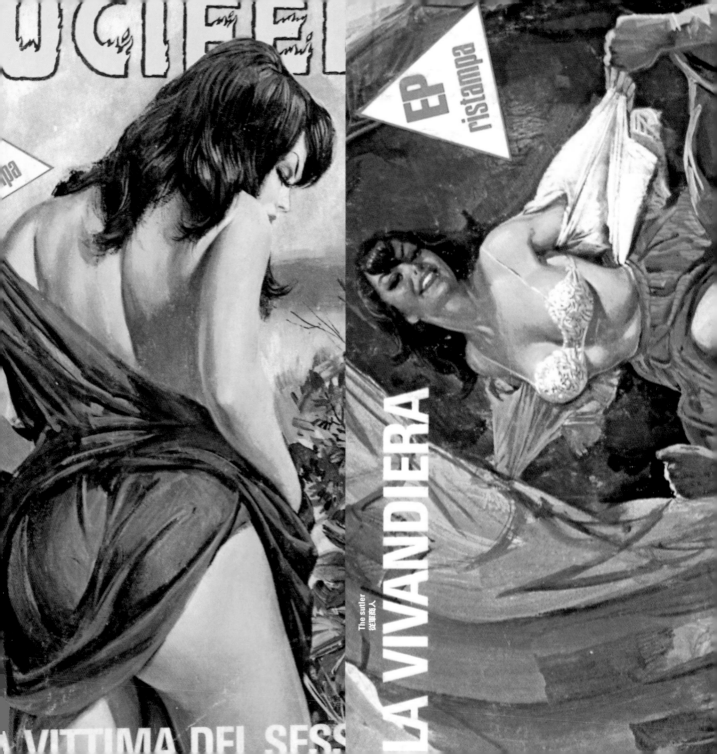

UCIFEL

EP ristampa

VITTIMA DEL SESS

LA VIVANDIERA

The sutler
従軍商人

EPA,
ADITORE !

Burn in hell, traitor!
裏切り者よ、地獄に堕ちろ

EP ristampa

LE SIRENE

2 EPISODI COMPLETI L. 400

FUMETT
PER ADULT
L. 200

BELGIO 20 FB
FRANCIA 2 F
GERMANIA 1,60 DI
INGHILTERRA 14 p
SVIZZERA 2 Fs.

VOGLIA ANTICA

2 EPISODI

Ancient lust
太古の色情

EP ristampa

VIETATO AI MINORI DI 18 ANNI

un milione
d'anni fa

A million years ago
百万年の昔

la valle

il guardia

The guardian
守衛

L. 300

CACCIA GROSSA

CERVELLO FINE

" Forest of the sleeping beauty "
Raganotto runs riot
『眠れる森の美女』放蕩のラガノット

RAGANOTTO
FA CASOTTO

SCO DELLA
ADDORMENTATA

Lady "Pleasure" Godeva
快楽婦人

LADY GODEVA

ATTUALITÀ

L. 1500

DONNA, SBIRRO

Blackmarket of wives
妻たちの闇市

IL MERC
CLANDES
DELLE M

PER
ADULTI

VIETATO
AI MINORI

Death of a nymphomaniac
ある淫乱女の死

MORTE
DI UNA
NINFOMANE

PROIBITA

ADULTI   AI MINORI

LUSSURIA
DI PADRE

" A father's lust "
When slapping her arse brings vile pleasure and depravity...
父親の欲望！娘の尻を叩くとき、劣情と堕落を呼び覚ます…

Quando
sculacciare
la figlia diventa
una turpe
occasione di
piacere e di
depravazione...

VIOLENTA

ALL'ULTIMO SANGUE

PERIODICO PER ADULTI

LENTA

IL DELITTO
ALLE CALCAGNA

"House of violence"
Torture and drugs for the "good of the soul" ...
Inmates of a fake safe house, stripped naked and enslaved

暴力の家!
「いつわり」のための拷問と麻薬。裸にされ奴隷とかした、
上辺だけの家庭の囚人

LA CASA DELLA VIOLENZA

torture e droga
per il bene dell'anima ...
spogliati di tutto e tenuti

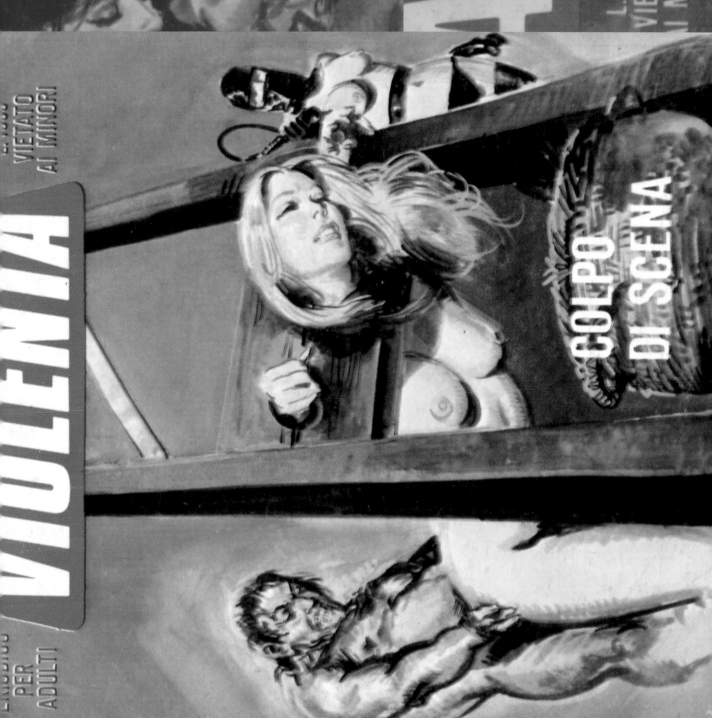

VIOLENTA

COLPO DI SCENA

GIALLA

CRIMEN
NEL
MONDO

L. 800
VIETATO
AI MINORI

SUD

PERIODICO
PER
ADULTI

L. 1000
VIETATO
AI MINORI

LA VENDETTA
DEL CORNUTO

Aria of death
死のアリア

PROIBITA

" Sexy-Radio-Taxi " Dilettante prostitutes offer erotic services by radio
『セクシー・ラジオ・タクシー』 スキモノ専用売春宅配サービス

SEXY-RADIO-TAXI

Battone dilettant
offrono
prestazioni
erotiche via radio

L. 800
VIETATO
AI MINORI

FEMMINA
AMBIGUA

ATTUALITÀ PROIBITA

PERIODICO PER ADULTI

L. 800 VIETATO AI MINORI

"Pig woman"
The vice of an eccentric pig-like billionairess
「豚女」 豚のような億万長者の悪徳

LA DONNA PORCO

DI TETTE

I vizi di una miliardaria eccentrica con sembianza suina

ATTUALITÀ PROIBITA

ODICO
ER
ULTI

L.700
VIETATO
AI MINORI

"Beautiful pig woman "
When sexual depravity leads to death ...
『美しき豚女』性の堕落が死を招く…

LA BELLA PORCA

Quando
la depravazione
sessuale conduce
alla morte...

Cayman woman
鰐女

LA
RAGAZZA
DEL KAIMANO

The depraved stepfather
継父の堕落

GIALLA
L. 700
VIETATO
COCKTAIL MORTALE

Lethal cocktail
死のカクテル

QUALITA

ITALIA

L. 700

NEL MONDO GIALLA VIETATO AI MINORI

Writhing of the vipers
身をくねらせる蝮

GROVIGLIO DI VIPERE

VIOLENTA

L. 1000
VIETATO
AI MINORI

Caress of the gravedigger
墓堀人の不覚

EZZA

CHINO

L. 1200
VIETATO
AI MINORI

IL NEGRO

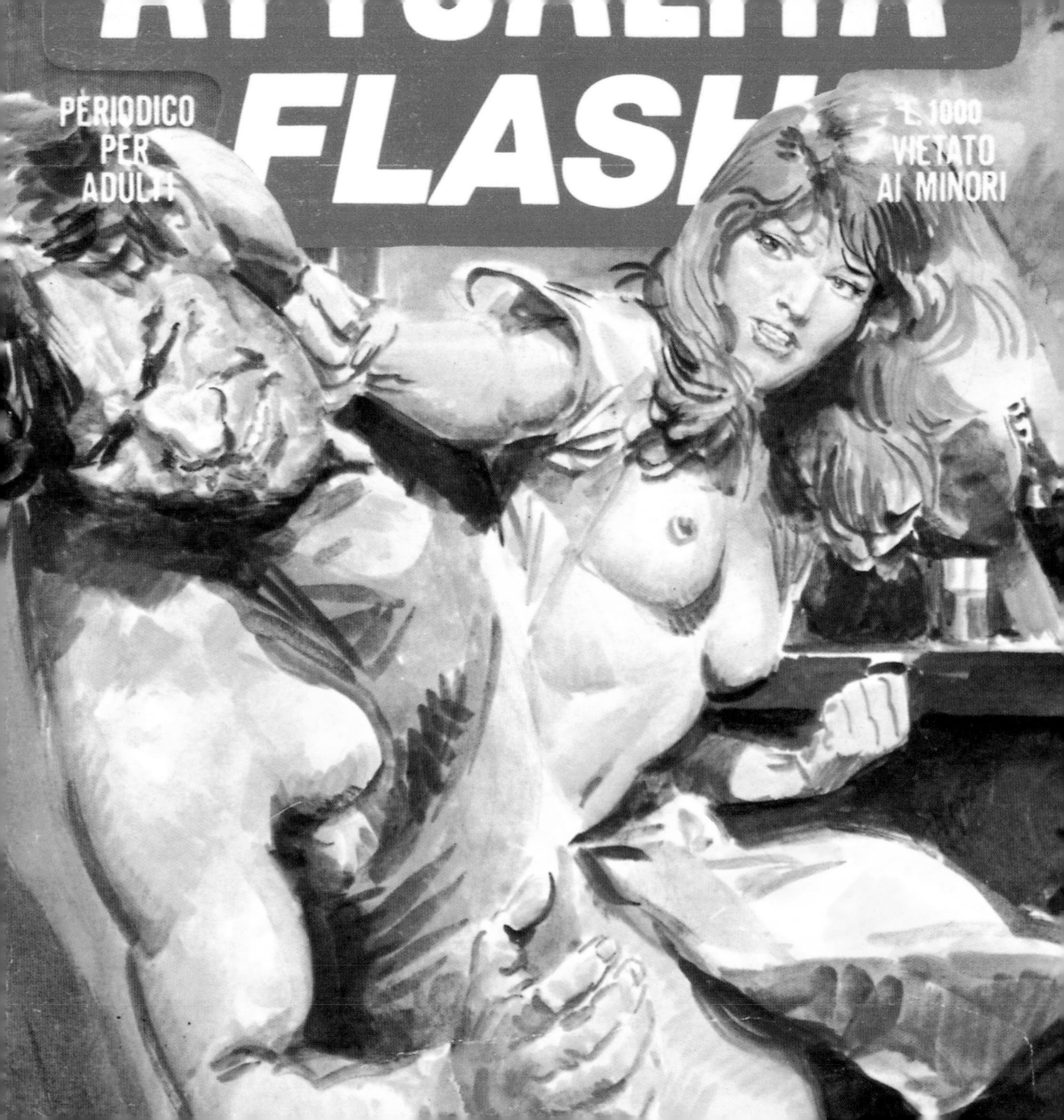
FLASH
PERIODICO PER ADULTI
L. 1000
VIETATO AI MINORI

Street Design File 16
Spaghetti EROTICO : Sex and Violence in Italian Comics
First Published in Japan 2001 by ASPECT Corp.
4-36-19 Yoyogi, Shibuya-ku, Tokyo, Japan 151-0053
telephone 81-3-5351-8607 fax 81-3-5351-8609
Text by Antonio Casilli
Translation by Alfred Birnbaum, Kyoichi Tsuzuki
Designed by Kyoko Fujisaki
Editor : Kyoichi Tsuzuki

All the comicbooks are private collection.

©Kyoichi Tsuzuki 2001
Printed and bound by Mitsumura Printing Co. Ltd., Tokyo
ISBN4-7572-0815-4

ストリート デザイン ファイル 16
Spaghetti EROTICO : イタリア式エログロ漫画館
2001年3月14日　第1版 第1刷発行
文　　　アントニオ・カッシーリ
翻訳　　アルフレッド・バーンバウム、都築響一
デザイン　藤崎匡子
編集　　都築響一
編集人　宮崎洋一
発行人　高比良公成
発行所　株式会社アスペクト
　　　　〒151-0053 東京都渋谷区代々木4-36-19
　　　　トーシンビルアネックス1F
　　　　[営業部] 電話　03-5351-8607
　　　　　　　　　FAX　03-5351-8609
印刷所　光村印刷株式会社